MY BIG FAMILY AT CHURCH

Written and Illustrated by
Helen Caswell

Abingdon Press
Nashville

Library of Congress Cataloging-in-Publication Data

Caswell, Helen Rayburn.
My big family at church / written and illustrated by Helen Caswell.
    p.   cm. — (Growing in faith series)
Summary: A young child describes the activities that take place at
church when people come together to show their love for God.
    ISBN 0-687-27533-4 (pbk. : alk. paper)
    1. Church—Juvenile literature. [1. Church.] I. Title.
II. Series.
BV600.2.C37   1989
264—dc19   88-30630
                                                                      CIP
                                                                       AC

MANUFACTURED IN HONG KONG

I like to go to church on Sunday morning.

All the church buildings are different.
Some have steeples pointing up to God,
and some have colored windows,
and some have bells ringing.

But each church is like a place
where a big family gets together.

My church family gets together every Sunday, and other days, too, to show God that we love him.

All sorts of people are in my church family.
Some make music for God.
I like to hear them singing.
I sing along:
Halleluja!
Amen!

Some teach Sunday school.
I like my teacher.
She tells us about camels
and good Samaritans
and Jesus.

Some people cook in the kitchen
when we have suppers for
our church family.
I like the chocolate cake.

Some of the people keep the church clean and beautiful. I like to pick up the papers near the sidewalk.

Some go out to visit people who are sick or need help, and we collect things—like my extra clothes and toys to send to people who need them.

The people in my church family
are all different,
but we all work together
and love each other,
because we love God.

And God promised a long time ago
that when people get together
to show their love for him,
he will come and be there with them.

God Must Like to Laugh
teaches children about God and the world God created.

I Know Who Jesus Is tells children about Jesus and his life.

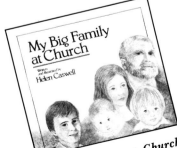

My Big Family at Church helps children understand church and why we go.

THE GROWING IN·FAITH LIBRARY

The Growing in Faith Library presents these beautifully illustrated books by Helen Caswell. They are designed to introduce children to six basic concepts of the Christian faith.

Also available is the **Guidebook for Adults**—for parents, grandparents, and teachers who love their three- to seven-year-olds and want them to grow in faith.

The **Guidebook** uses each of the six books to

- Address children's questions
- Identify teachable moments
- Give additional ideas to help children grow in faith

I Can Talk with God shows children how they can pray and listen to God.

God's Love Is for Sharing explains how we can share God's love with others.

God Is Always with Me helps children understand eternal life.